Contents

Page

Weblink: www.curriculumvisions.com

Moving about

There are many ways to move in the playground.

You can see here how many ways of moving about there are in a playground.

Each time we move we need to push or pull ourselves.

This girl is going down a slide.

This boy is pulling himself up a climbing frame.

CurriculumVisions  1E Science@School

Pushes and pulls

Peter Riley and Dr Brian Knapp

Curriculum Visions

Science@School

Teacher's Guide
There is a Teacher's Guide available
to accompany this book.

Dedicated Web Site
There is a wealth of supporting
material including videos and activities
available at the Professional Zone,
part of our dedicated web site:

www.CurriculumVisions.com

The Professional Zone
is a subscription zone.

A CVP Book.
First published in 2008

Authors
*Peter Riley, BSc, C Biol, MI Biol, PGCE,
and Brian Knapp, BSc, PhD*

Senior Designer
Adele Humphries, BA, PGCE

Educational Consultant
*Jan Smith (former Deputy Head of Wellfield School,
Burnley, Lancashire)*

Editor
Gillian Gatehouse

Designed and produced by
EARTHSCAPE

Printed in China by
WKT Co., Ltd

**Curriculum Visions Science@School
Volume 1E Pushes and pulls**
*A CIP record for this book is available
from the British Library.*
ISBN: 978 1 86214 257 2

Picture credits
All pictures are from the Earthscape and
ShutterStock collections.

*This product is manufactured from sustainable
managed forests. For every tree cut down at least one
more is planted.*

To make a bicycle move, you push
on the pedals with your feet.

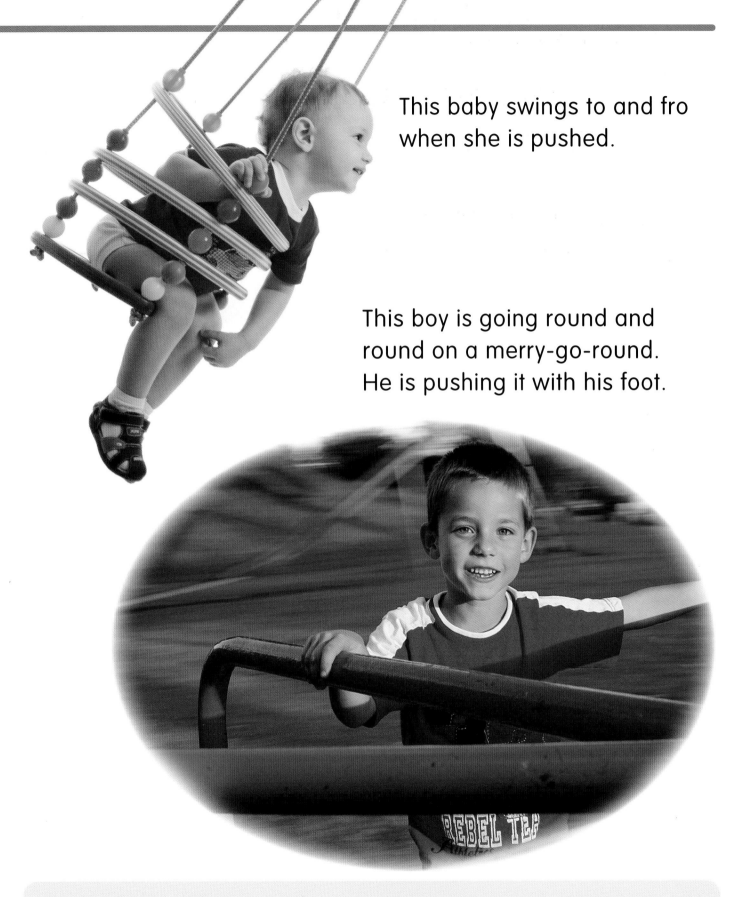

This baby swings to and fro when she is pushed.

This boy is going round and round on a merry-go-round. He is pushing it with his foot.

How many different ways do you move in a playground?

Weblink: www.curriculumvisions.com

How we move

We can move in many ways.

We can walk.

We can run.

We can lift our arms.

We can hop.

We can swim.

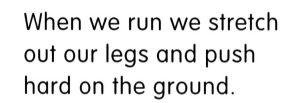

When we run we stretch out our legs and push hard on the ground.

When we swim we stretch out our arms and legs.

When we jump we spring up.

Weblink: www.curriculumvisions.com

When we skip we jump and move our hands in a circle.

When we play hopscotch we use our feet to spring up.

How many different ways can you move about?

Weblink: www.curriculumvisions.com

Muscles and moving

Muscles move our bodies.

Our bodies have muscles.

You can feel them in your arms and legs.

We use our muscles to move our bodies.

Muscles in your face
make you smile.

We can feel the muscles between our hands and our shoulders go tight when we lift something heavy.

muscles

Muscles in your arms show up if you hold heavy weights.

muscles

Can you make the muscles in your neck nod your head?

Weblink: www.curriculumvisions.com

Pushing

We can move things when we push them.

You push a pram.

We use many words for pushing.

We can say squeezing.

We can say pressing.

We can say punching.

We can say tapping.

We can say squashing.

You push your teeth together when you eat. You squash your fingers together to hold the sandwich.

You tap a key when you use a computer.

You push down on the handle to open the door.

You push your toothbrush up and down when you clean your teeth.

Do you push a ball when you kick it?

Weblink: www.curriculumvisions.com

Pulling

We can move things when we pull them.

We use many words for pulling.

We pick things up.

We lift things.

We carry things.

We drag things.

We stretch things.

We tug things.

We rip things.

We can pick chocolates from a box.

A horse pulls a carriage.

Weblink: www.curriculumvisions.com

sled

Parents pull a sled.

We lift shopping into the car.

A boy tugs
on a rope.

**When you put your socks on
do you pull or push them?**

Stopping

Moving things can stop slowly or quickly.

It is easy to stop small things moving.
You can stop a ball quickly.

It is hard to stop large things.
A train is large. It cannot stop quickly.

A lorry is a large thing.
It cannot stop quickly.

When cars travel slowly they can stop in a shorter distance.

You can stop a ball quickly because it is small.

An amber light on its own tells cars to get ready to stop.

What rules do you know for crossing the road safely?

Weblink: www.curriculumvisions.com

Changing speed

Things can **speed up and slow down.**

We often change how fast we move. This is called changing speed.

If you start to run to get to a class on time you speed up.

If you put on the brakes of your bicycle you slow down.

A bicycle will stop slowly if you put the brakes on gently.

You change speed all the time on a roller coaster.

As you reach the top you slow down.

As you leave the top you speed up.

Do you speed up as you go up a roller coaster, or when you come down?

Wind and water

Wind and water push on things and make them move.

The wind makes a kite fly. It makes a ship sail.

A very strong wind is called a hurricane. It can knock over trees and houses.

Moving water is very powerful, too.

The wind makes a flag flutter.

A hurricane smashes up houses.

The wind makes the sails push the ship forwards.

A fast river carries these canoeists along.

Moving water makes a waterwheel turn.

What happens to trees when the wind pushes on them?

Weblink: www.curriculumvisions.com

Movement and play

You use pushes and pulls when you play.

Every time you play with a toy, you are pulling or pushing it.

Every time you make a sandcastle on the beach, you pull and push the sand.

You push down on the jack-in-a-box to make it jump up.

You make a sandcastle by pushing the sand about.

You make a train move by pushing it along the track.

A puppet moves when you pull the strings.

You make bubbles by blowing (pushing) them.

What pushes and pulls do you make when you play with your toys?

Words to learn

10

Brakes

The part of a bicycle or car that slows it down.

brake

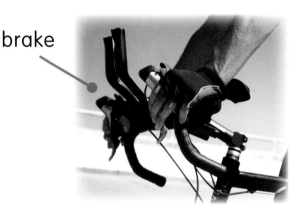

Canoeist

A person who uses a canoe and paddle to move through water.

Hopscotch

A hopping game using squares marked on the ground.

Jack-in-a-box

A doll on a spring in a box. It pops out when the box lid is opened.

Weblink: www.curriculumvisions.com

Kite

A toy made from thin material which goes up in the wind and is held by a string.

Merry-go-round

A roundabout. You go round and round on it when someone pushes you.

Rollercoaster

A carriage which moves on a track with bends and loops in it.

Waterwheel

A wheel turned by water. As the wheel turns it works machines.

Weblink: www.curriculumvisions.com

Index